THE FARM

ALL KINDS OF FARMS

Ann Larkin Hansen
ABDO & Daughters

Published by Abdo & Daughters, 4940 Viking Drive, Suite 622, Edina, Minnesota 55435.

Copyright © 1996 by Abdo Consulting Group, Inc., Pentagon Tower, P.O. Box 36036, Minneapolis, Minnesota 55435 USA. International copyrights reserved in all countries. No part of this book may be reproduced in any form without written permission from the publisher.

Printed in the United States.

Cover Photo credits: Peter Arnold, Inc.
Interior Photo credits: Peter Arnold, Inc.

Edited by Bob Italia

Library of Congress Cataloging-in-Publication Data

Hansen, Ann Larkin.
   All Kinds of Farms / Ann Larkin Hansen
    p. cm. -- (The Farm)
   Includes index.
   Summary: Describes what farms are like, how they differ from one another, and
   why many middle-sized farms are disappearing.
    ISBN 1-56239-621-8
   1. Agriculture--Juvenile literature. 2. Farms--Juvenile literature.   [1. Agriculture 2. Farms.]
   I. Title. II. Series: Hansen, Ann Larkin. Farm.
   S519.H3725 1996   96-11093
   630'.973--dc20   CIP
                                                                              AC

About the Author

Ann Larkin Hansen has a degree in history from the University of St. Thomas in St. Paul, Minnesota. She currently lives with her husband and three boys on a farm in northern Wisconsin, where they raise beef cattle, chickens, and assorted other animals.

Contents

Farms Grow Food

A farm is a piece of land which is used to raise plants and animals to eat or sell. Farms grow everything from apricots to watermelons, and from turkeys to ostriches.

Every farm is different. Some are tucked on the sides of hills and surrounded by woods. Others sprawl over thousands of **acres**. But every farm is busy, raising the food we eat each day.

Opposite page:
Harvesting crops
in Montana.

How Farms
Have Changed

Before there were superhighways and
refrigerator trucks, most food was grown close to
where it was eaten. Each farm had to grow many
different things. Most farms had cows, pigs,
chickens, a big garden, fruit trees, and several
different fields.

Today, any food can be kept cold and trucked
across the country. Most food is raised where the
weather and **soil** are best for that plant or animal.
Then it is trucked to stores everywhere. Most farms
raise only one or two things. Many have no animals
at all!

Opposite page:
This horse-drawn wagon is
a rare sight on today's farms.

Big Farms

In 1935, there were 6.8 million farms in the United States. Today, there are less than two million farms. But about the same amount of land is being farmed. The farms have just gotten much, much bigger.

In many areas, middle-sized farms are disappearing. When farmers retire or quit, they sell their land to a neighbor. Now, the neighbor's farm is twice as big, and there is one farm instead of two.

A large cotton farm in Mississippi.

Little Farms

Not all farms are getting bigger. There are many small pieces of land that old farmers won't sell, or big farmers don't want. These little farms are used for **crops** that don't take much space, like **herbs**. Farmers with other jobs will work part-time on a little farm.

Many beef cattle and **organic** vegetables are raised by part-time farmers. The little farms grow things that big farms ignore. We need big and little farms to grow all the different foods we like to eat.

Opposite page:
A farm with geese
and squash in Iowa.

What Farms Are Like

Farms are busy and sometimes not very neat. Animals must be fed every day. Machinery seems to always need fixing. There are fences to mend and fields to plow.

Farms are full of feed buckets and tools. Tractors and **implements** roar in and out of the yard. Dogs and cats keep an eye on the action. Sheds and old **haystacks** line edges of the property. There are all sorts of things to explore and do on the farm.

Tomato harvesting on an Ohio farm.

Why Farms Grow Different Crops

Every animal and plant has certain things it likes best. **Cattle** enjoy cool weather and plenty of grass. Chickens like hot weather and lots of grain to eat. Corn needs rich **soil** and lots of rain. Potatoes need lighter soil and cooler weather.

In the United States, the Northeast is cool and rainy. The Southeast is hot and wet. The **plains states** are dry, and California is warm and dry. Each region **specializes** in different **crops**, so farms in each area are different.

A grain field in the Texas panhandle.

Farms of the Northeast

Much of the land in the northeastern states is hilly. When the first settlers came, the land was covered with woods. The trees had to be cut down and the stumps burned. It was hard work to farm the steep hills. Farms were small and close together.

Today, most of these farms are forest again. But the old farmhouses and small barns are still tucked behind every hill. Some fields are used for **specialty crops**, like vegetables and **herbs**. Sheep and cows still graze the small pastures.

Northeastern states

A farm in Vermont.

Dairy Farms

Millions of dairy cows graze the gentle hills of states like Wisconsin, New York, and Pennsylvania. The barns on these farms are big enough to hold 50 or 100 cows. Most have **silos** standing next to them, full of chopped corn. The fields grow corn, hay, and oats. There are plenty of sheds full of machinery, lots of gardens, and apple trees in the yards.

From one dairy farm you can usually see other farms because they are not too big or far apart. Often there is a tire swing on an old tree in the front yard.

Wisconsin

New York

Pennsylvania

Opposite page: A corn crib on a dairy farm in Iowa.

Corn, Soybeans, and Hogs

The richest, flattest land in the country is found in the Midwest. There is enough rain and heat to grow miles and miles of corn and soybeans. The farms are far apart, and successful enough to have new houses. The only trees are near the farmhouses.

The machinery in the Midwest is much bigger, and the sheds are huge. There may be a barn and **silo** for beef **cattle**. Pigs are raised in long, low sheds. But many farmers have no animals at all. Instead of feeding beef and pigs all winter, they go on vacation!

Midwestern states

View of a farm in southern Wisconsin.

Way Out West

The farther west you go, the drier it becomes. Only wheat grows well there. But it takes a lot of land to grow enough wheat for a farmer to make a living. Dryland wheat farms are huge. So is the machinery that tends the fields.

Farther west, not even wheat can grow. This is ranch country, and **cattle** have to walk far to find enough grass to eat. Ranchers use horses and pickup trucks to keep track of the cows. The ranch houses are surrounded by low barns and **corrals**.

The far western states.

A wheat harvest in Colfax, Washington.

Irrigation

When **irrigating**, the farmer takes underground or river water and uses it on the **crops**. This is done when there is not enough rain. Because of irrigation, California and dry areas of the Southwest can grow fruit, vegetables, and rice all year round.

Many of these crops must be picked by hand. Farms in this area may have many little houses for the extra workers to live in during harvest season. There are plenty of sheds for sorting and storing the crops.

Irrigation fields in northern California.

25

All Kinds of Farms

No two farms are alike. You never know exactly what you will find. There may be a stream running through the yard, and new calves in the barn. There may be miles of wheat turning gold in the setting sun. There may be catfish ponds, horses being trained, or huge machines picking cotton.

No matter what a farm looks like, it is working to grow food. There is always fresh air and plenty to do.

Opposite page:
Dumping cut grass
for the compost.

Glossary

acre (AY-kurr)—a square piece of land that measures 202 feet (62 m) on each side.

cattle—animals of the ox family, such as cows, bulls and steers, raised for meat and dairy products.

compost—a mixture of decayed organic matter that is used for fertilizer.

corral—a fenced enclosure for cattle or horses.

crop—the plants or animals raised for sale.

farm—any place that produces more than $1,000 worth of agricultural products in one year.

haystack—a large pile of hay.

herbs—plants usually used to add taste to other foods. Common herbs are parsley, basil, and oregano.

hogs—pigs.

implements—machinery towed behind a tractor to perform many jobs in the field. Common implements are plows, haybines, and forage choppers.

irrigation—underground or river water pumped to a farm to water crops.

organic—growing plants or animals without using any man-made chemicals.

plains states—rolling, treeless country west of the Mississippi.

silo—tall, tubular structure of concrete or metal (some old ones were wood) used to store chopped plants for animal feed.

soil—part of the Earth's surface that plants are grown in; dirt.

specialize—to raise just one or two things instead of many different plants and animals.

Index